THE WALK OF ABSENCE

THE WALK OF ABSENCE

ERBA

gnOme

The Walk of Absence
© the author and gnOme books

2016

gnOme books
gnomebooks.wordpress.com

Please address inquiries to:
gnomebooks@gmail.com

Cover image: Caspar David Friedrich, Monk by the Sea,
public domain image.
https://en.wikipedia.org/wiki/The_Monk_by_t
he_Sea#/media/File:Caspar_David_Friedrich_ -
_Der_M%C3%B6nch_am_Meer_-
_Google_Art_Project.jpg

ISBN-13: 978-0692660454
ISBN-10: 0692660453

LUPARA

Autumn's purling lament
was shattered
by my mother's wailing
this year

And oh the lullabies
Agape the lullabies froze spellbound
like crows suspended in their flight
as her song rose sharp as a knife
slashing across the air
across void and world alike
finding no obstacle
to resist its beauty

Have your mothers ever sung thus for you?
All of space is torn and night bleeds
lupine through its wounds
The moon
The moon's deranged
It does not show the way
and the stars are all misplaced

Unstrung
from doleful togetherness,
the townspeople are alone
No eulogies, no panegyric praise.

Unhinged
and writhing, like a severed snake,
the black cortege now brings no solace
in solemn poise, in measured step,
and one by one
a town empties,
a crowd's undone.

Thus fell wintry silence,
and settled, white like snow,
on your hair, on your hands,
on the long untrodden step of our door.

BEYOND COLLAPSE

A lone shadow stretches soundlessly
out of the woods carrying a stark naked
waxen figure or draggling it behind,
which it buries in the sand or
lets sink into the lake
before lying down, there,
at the blackest speck of night, as coarse
outline of exhaustion,
for there are more corpses deep
inside the forest, out of which
it claimed this one, grotesque
countenance like the rest
coupled with an unpronounceable name,
oblivious of whether it was the right one
among the heap of nameless dead
from whom none emerged victorious...

GRANDFATHER'S FOREBODING
(WHEN OUR CHILDREN...)

At daybreak, the evidence of night's murderous celebration
appears limp and helpless on the dank sidewalk
outside my window as I wake to the unstoppable chant,
God is greatest, God is most merciful... There is no god
but God...

The depots are on fire and war wages blithely on
from neighborhood to neighborhood
as entranced we run wild in the streets;
God is greatest, God is merciful...

Our joy is fierce
for there is a hidden sorrow deep in every joy
thence hungry, barefoot, and free
our children coldly hold us blameless
for their past helplessness...

FRANKINCENSE

> *My daydream. I drew near*
> *and whispered slowly*
> *in your ear. I said,*
> *These words shall never be spoken,*
> *and we will not meet*
> *but in another dream.*

I said that I left
and never spoke to her.
I ransacked her black eyes to ensure
that there may still be tears.
As I walked away I said to myself,
the deadliest stab of regret
does not come from fighting and falling,
but from never having fought at all.
Walking away I saw my generation rolling
without a trace... and on the way back
I passed not through rubble but
through the indifference of things changed,
the cool radiant tepidness
of "life goes on,"
and smuggled in the grievous dagger
of memory...

> *(I came to you in my burning nights,*
> *in my reveries, and in my unquenchable thirst*
> *my delirium became ...)*

I said that I left
and never spoke to her.
She asked, why did you not come to me?
I said, so that I may still have tears.
Silently, I said. Do not wait for me—
your entire life is waiting.
Do not whisper the meeting place—
I know where all lovers meet,
and I will find you in the end,
as widowed you sit on the lonely bench,
at the foot of the hills,
under the pine tree,

by the side of the lake...
knitting, old and wrinkled...

You remembered our vows
and smiled with your wrinkles.
You came, you said soundlessly.
I said, I came so I may give you back
your tears
and the promise of the unreal ...
There we sat in our dewdrop well,
And without words we spoke
of eternity and its craze ...

Still she is wrapped
in her marriage and forgetful memories
and only half of this is true;
the unspoken...
so that the longing...
so that the dream, the ache, the falling...

a call like this...

REVERBERATION

At the bottom of my glass
I search for my green fairy

> Out of the deep unrippled calm, my beyond,
> her eye silently answers me...
> ———

If only I could hear your voice once again
singing to the lacerating tune...

> Silently, she answers me,
> because all longing is silent...

I want to know,
I want to know whether I have ever existed.
Whether from your tears
this drink filled for me...
Or am I drinking someone else's glass?

IN THE BUTTERFLY FOREST
behind the oak tree
I saw your wondrous eye
intently watching me
and I followed
like an explorer or a hunter.
I, your crevice
dreamt of losing myself
in your fullness...

You are my lungs...
and I, your unreality

Your fear was justified:
this realm of aught and naught
cannot endure the fire
that craves for the ashes
beyond your all or nothing.

FROM ANZIO

I sent you a storm today,
melody and fire,
instead of the lackadaisical letter,
for words are wasteful,
and terribly ambiguous
to express my turbulence...

O child of old age,
The roads of your capital
are muddy today
in the maelstrom
of my doldrums and tantrums.

Inexpugnable city...
What is this breath that burns through you
when you look in the eye of the storm?
Is that a madness reflected in your eyes?
Is it my madness?

O love!
How adorable you look
with my fire inside you,
and you forget your subjects
and possessions,
moved by an illusion.

AT THE GALLOWS

Beyond loss, survival, and restful suicide,
beyond victory and defeat
there is us

hanging above the spellbound onlookers' heads
who hypnotized follow the illaqueating swings of our bodies
and their immovable gesture toward absence

MISALIGNED

I wrote of smoking a cigarette once,
near the window watching the street lights sliding under
the rain, elongating like the limbs of lovers
the last night before saying goodbye...
I watched quivering life outside and smoked
it unto death, longing, like the dying solder
taking a last drag...

I wrote of my namesake
by the ruins of a school wall after the bombing,
wet to the bone, slowly walking as if lost
under the mantle of damp thoughts,
contrived memories surrounding him
in a fluttering death-dance, drowning
in happiness of brief existence, erased
by an invisible hand...

I wrote of the girl by the window
breathing on the windowpane;
The window's high against the sky
and drawing figures with her finger,
smiling, as I passed by...
(Was she smiling at me or the figures
on the window?)

I wrote this...
A late response to tell to another girl,
in another wet street in a city of sliding lights,
as she sleeps and doesn't hear...

IMAGELESS

In your solitude the world rests
agape and endless
night falls
in love
with your oblivion...

In this eye-gauging night there
are no stars
no moon
to keep you company only
the soot wooly deafness of their consumed past
without narrative...

SAVAGE GAMES OF AXE AND FIRE

With fondness I remember the gatherings of days past...
a blackened boughless tree leaning against the rubble of the old
    house,
reminiscing about the ancient forest...

Blood. O my blood.
Was the love of this lonely stump too great for you?

None is my blood! Forlorn.
The grievous skies are barren and the earth
once an indomitable mare stands ravaged...

The forests, singed hair upon a black woman's back
for our brotherhood was forged
through the ceremony of the accelerating atoms.

Aye, we burned with love, my brothers and I...
our love icy, winterkill, perpendicular as we fell
fulgent through nights crowded with overlapping shadows
rising, while the earth slid imperceptibly as if on an oily
railroad toward darker spaces...

My darling ones,
In your slumber, do you dream
of new worlds and savage games of axe and fire?

I dream of new worlds.

For surely, I am now an incinerated forest,
and even the tightrope o'er the abyss is far from me...
a blotching wound swirling black on the earth's skin
copulating with the desiccating winds. Betorn,
I am the black ashes dancing
in the blinking eye of these empty days' passing.

PSALMS

For the passing of things, fullness and solitude...
For distance, coldness and yearning...
For erasure, affliction and forgetfulness...
For the expectant, the deliverance of the cruel song...

For the forest, stillness and the pursuit...
For midnight... intimacy and murder...
For the passionate kiss, the softness of lips and the threat of..
For the quidnunc, the sweet dandle of the accursed song...

For the haunting, disappearance and lingering...
For the doom, the alcove and the relic...
For the frozen hand, the blank sheet and the dried pen...
For me, for you, the choked song...

MY HOMELAND

A shot pierced through the heart
of silence,
reverberating through its paleness, a white shroud
in the wind.

Then, the fusillade tore into its enclosures,
unfolding buds,
and the tang of gunpowder impregnated
every flower.

The sky darkened as birds
rose
in flustered togetherness, like a
black forest
leaving its home, and silence sprawled
once more.

UNDER SHADING HAVEN

On Monday, under shading haven
of the great palm tree
where for the first time we kissed,
or church-days, in grandmother's creaky room
where jolted in violent embrace
our warm perspiring skin
cared not for the ancient chill

and stealing under the bedsheets
where our enflamed breaths caressed our faces
and intoxicated us, and blood, sweat and tears of joy
assuaged our criminal thirst
and longing

we the desert wild winds
became the bane of this town...

THE PROMISE

Could one word have saved you, love?
You who are so young and melancholy,
could one dusty word have rescued you
as you sat there growing old
in your rocking chair, with your madness
weaving webs upon torn webs,
unaware of your resentment?

Could a word whispered hurriedly
and in one breath into your ear,
already fugitive and forever out of time,
have reclaimed you, there, where
the fragile promise of the elliptical is met
with the stultifying insanity of the familiar?

There is a rift between us.
So we sat there, mute,
without a word of consolation,
hurt and bewildered...

What else remains?
You, that have your whole life ahead of you,
can you rise above your history,
abandon your preordained future
and cease concerning yourself with your death?
Your death.

They say your death is not in vain,
and that by it we both gain;
You, the freedom from yourself,
I, the renewal of my pain.
−And they? Have they nothing at stake?

You're wounded my love, lying in their mud
and still asking,
with blood in your mouth, asking,
exhausted, alone and isolated, yet hoping,
questioning, but waiting...

Is there time?
Do we still have time
to dance through all the steps of
this same drab beat before we fall to war?
Give me your hand and your heart of ice at once.
We must cut out our tongues
and fall to war without
another breath,
or sound...

THE PASSAGE

A heightened narrowness
through which shafts of darkened luminescence
march upon the two dimensional plane of invasion
as immanent reconfigurations of falling and standing...

As black rank and file of a blank realm
they appear after we are gone...
We are forbidden! We are forbidden!
A voice echoes in the dank corridors of forgetfulness...

Ancient stratagems that find a way for the unthought
quicken their pace even in the absence of space
forever perspiring in search of motion where all is still
and where the frost only, urges us on...

THE ADVENT

[CHAMBER I]

Transfixed
Emptiness gnaws at my chest
harrowing maddening arcs of escape
as the familiarity of objects turns
oppressive

Incomprehensible
desire for my absence
fills the room with
hostility

Distant
panting waves wrought
on the world's contorted walls
usher forth the age of the
drought

Inhumed
From unfathomable depths
an irrepressible sob
breaks surging
through trachea to larynx urging
forth an inexperienced
cry

Agape
My mouth hurts
my ears and my ears
hurt my whole being that
splits apart like a cracked
seed in springtime

The darkness...
then, the lightning...

[DECLENSION I]

DEEP FISSURE

Quiescent,
anchor and ship.
The earth's asleep.

Wide-awake,
like rift
across the totality of her dream,
trails the road of devastation.

[CHAMBER II]

You were asleep
the evening I was abduced
into your world.

Towards dawn you woke,
and we embraced for the first time
after our separation.
But I no longer trusted your embraces.

You brought me into your world
order in order
to forget me in our wedding day's
unctuous embrace.

Then, walled yourself in
under the shadow of my absence
that you worshipped
like a holy stone, and covered
with the silken veil
of a thousand prayer-like
black kisses.

And we danced in our own awkward way.
You circumambulated counterclockwise
around my stillness
until you collapsed, then began anew...

Your cycles are a bracelet around
my ankle, my ankle
a tree stump
whose ring-rust furrows count
the earth's counter revolutions, whose amputated branches
hold the weight of heaven...

My ankle is a tree stump.
Barkless.
The color of human skin.
In darkling night, at languishing dawn,
glittering obscene...

[DECLENSION II]

TWO-STRIKE

Shifting allegiance,
a time born old here
bows
to another master

Empty, her grimace
impales on the double
as destiny
trembles, outnumbered...

[CHAMBER III]

Like sickly leaves the centuries drooped and fell
overburdened
by your writings and your history...

You conjured up the Enlightenment and Ragnarök,
the last battle that never occurred...
Do you still seek to know? and what?

...this is the moment of impending doom and everlasting
deferment, awaiting for the remnants of old destiny's tale
to fulfill their oath, on the morrow...

...the dregs of time are destiny, and the great slaughter
is postponed as pulverulent grey old men, squatting 'round
the abattoir, raise toasts to longevity and good health...

...syncopic modern sacrifices, the days rustle by shambling
through attic trapdoors, guarding all that's dear
in yellowed ancient photo-album boxes...

...the prosopopoeia of pain sidles in dark dreams,
lingering concealed, like a yearned for phantom limb,
no longer allowed to hurt, or exist...

and the asylums are watchtowers, marking
the edge of the city, extending insane reason
to gratuitous affliction...

[DECLENSION III]

RAT-HORSES

Rabid, mooneyed, roughshod
horses black.
Dust-swirls, invisible riders
on their back.

Pumpjack, ratheads rock
the ground.
Thirsty birds scream above blisteringly
sweeping down.

[CHAMBER IV]

Al-'umm al-jāfiya! This is the age of
sequacity and painless birth.
The days are uneventful, and like beggars
the children are ungrateful...

You blessed the world ad absurdum.

No space is left. The paths of life are now paved.
The seeds of your blessings are strewn far and wide
upon concrete earth, and my brothers have all perished
as armed with your blessings they made their way
to where below is brighter than above.
For we had lit the earth on fire to conquer the sky...

No. Neither Earth nor Sky; the Tundra sheltered us;
Fire and ice; we were molded by the raging storm,
and unstoppable like weather, adust we rose
blotting out the sun...

O Mother of Titans. Good news from the North!
My brothers have perished...

So, let the song begin,
let the sorrow of the world begin its wailing song,
that the sky may be wept dry for
earth and earth
rise upwards
in flames...

Then, we shall return...
We shall rain down on you like grief,
like ashes,
like fistfuls of hair
pulled out of a mourning woman's head...

Smiling miles of calculative whirlwinds
out of hollow eye sockets, we shall arrive,
astride wild and terrifying hobbyhorses,
raucous, joyous, and deranged,
riding the winds of change, the winds of pestilence,
across all shadows, seas, and lands...

[DECLENSION IV]

AWAKE

The dust
dances violently at the gut-wrenching thud
of a thousand hooves approaching
in concentric dreamwaves.

An axe
thrust from beyond the ravine
of mist that divides sleep from waking,
with deadly intent,
awakes you.

[CHAMBER V]

Like a newborn screaming
when hurled into the horror of existence,
in freefall crossing from dreamworld to real world
in panic and unfurled,
for dear life holding on,
body turning like a leaf to face the fall
as it goes through spatial chambers
like a bullet through the wall,
with each level waking up
a little more...

Until,
reaching the bottom of the dream
with a thud,
or the mattress of the real,
oh, you die in your sleep
and sigh thus...
with relief.

THE WALK OF ABSENCE

CUMULATIVE LOSS

('With every birth,
more is lost.
Where does existence
pour its sorrows, and its hopes?—'
'Into the void.')

Is it possible that
Death
was taken away
at birth? or that birth
was always lost,
in death?

[I]

Is it possible that
death was taken from me
at birth? or that my
birth was always lost,
in death?

Through unfettered memories, under
the fustian, to the quiddity, I retraced my steps...

My birthplace has vanished.

From the grumbling bowels of want,
on terrible timeless bridges,
a nameless child
plays with pebbles in the dusk,
and names each one
according to some unknown rule.

He gives me a name and throws
me to my
rightful place
in the midst of a thousand nations
singing songs of belonging...

I am forgotten.

My erasures are memoried and light
grants me a face, bestows a
me upon my
face.

Millions upon millions we
await
the appointed hour when time will cease
to exist;

Under the sun we
sweat,
as the master silverhair
tans our backs
with his golden stingrays;

On the shore we
rest
while the waves wash out all
traces of our labour, and
every Sunday becomes
Doomsday.

My days are darkened.

The sun a puncture
in my eye
hatching dark spots on all
my gaze falls...

At night, I see
a formless crack in the ceiling,
and enter
the world of fantasy.

[II]

I followed your eye, Night
and your rusted eyelashes blinded me
with their beauty...

And your murmurs were sown into my head
like half heard words from an old poem,
or a long forgotten childhood song
wafted asudden through the forest
to resound once more.

And blindly I approached,
but you ebbed and scornfully asked:
Is every naught a dreamscape?

Then, I fell
and groped your darkness with my hands;
then, clutched your irradiant waves
your waves like a mare's fine hair, and
you flowed, and lovingly
and lovingly wailed...

[III]

Embraced
In your echo and
Solitude

Silence

Silence drips down
From quarters unknown

One drop

One drop in which
You can drown.

(For you are not a wolf
And cannot respond...)

[IV]

O fulvous Moon.
The only one that listens to my howl!

Sometimes I think, you were born
Of my howl tearing down the night's calm veil,
As the robe of the traveler is torn
By the thornbush, and spattered with his blood.

And when under the black rags of night
He struggles to cover his name and
His nakedness, your nakedness
Unforgivingly smothers his shame.

For through his wound alone,
Is he connate with you—
An intermittent bloodline;
One lost, another forged anew.

Of the traveler,
A drifter; of the drifter,
A lover; of the lover,
A killer... a murderer's

So the night glows,
Joyous,
Bleeding
Outside my barred window,
As my lover's face draws nearer...

In her face the auburn sky
Rippled,
Flowing,
Embraces the earth, erasing
Every outline...

[V]

Eyes shut
and a heart outside
its chest beeps to the right.

Plastic veins
extend
from the shrouded bed:

Refused rest/
Like the iris, whiteness
valvates...

I awake,
and the deluge has passed.
Is this reality? (I await).

[VI]

The nurse performs her duties,
at once attentive and disdainful,
like a goddess, unaffected
by the sorrows of existence.

Every new year's eve for a thousand years
she's measured my pulse,
and as the softest breeze her hair
falls on my face
setting it ablaze...

All this is familiar.
Yet, these memories do not belong to me...
For my life is a story whose narrators
are long dead...
And these moments are not recollections of the past
but an eroded present...

A memory or a dream
swaying what is
like rattling trees.

[VII]

The past too invited me to lie
down in its immutable depths, but I had
grown too large for its valleys, and my outstretched limbs
extended to unknown regions.

I saw my children's future
death,
and wept
as if it had already occurred.

I remembered my father,
his two departures one
after the other...

and mother, how you left
pieces of you on the road
before your firstborn came
to be the house of your dreams
six feet under.

and there you gathered your bones
over tarot cards, and began
dismantling the present
to read the past again.

Your labours mother, are in vain.
Your womb a barren memory
meticulously knitted into history
with many aglets and eyelets...

You never fully trusted me because of my blindness...
I am not the fabric. I am not the cloth, garment,
patches...
I am the wimble in your hand that you did not beget

[VIII]

Between eternity and here
    my hours
    ride on disappearance's horseback...

From birthplace to grave
    their gallop erases every history
    and Motherland...

My clock is permeated by nowhere...

Its pain is mute.
    It does not respond intelligibly
    to articulations of your pain.

From dust to breath to gasping clay,
    a desiccating wind without genealogy or lineage
    trails through everything...

Here, the walk of absence

    A strike that does not remember
        the rocks
    A spark that cannot recollect
        the strike
    A fire with no memory of
        the spark
    The ashes that have forgotten
        their former body

Other titles from gnOme

A & N • *Autophagiography*

Brian O'Blivion • *Blackest Ever Hole*

Cergat • *Earthmare: The Lost Book of Wars*

Eva Clanculator • *Atheologica Germanica*

Ars Cogitanda • *footnote to* silence

Pseudo-Leopardi • *Cantos for the Crestfallen*

M • *Un-Sight/ Un-Sound (delirium X.)*

M.O.N. • *ObliviOnanisM*

I. P. Snooks • *Be Still, My Throbbing Tattoo*

Subject A • *Verses from the Underlands*

Rasu-Yong Tugen, Baroness De Tristeombre • *Songs from the Black Moon*

Y.O.U. • *How to Stay in Hell*

Adrian Xavier, trans. • *The Lost Couplets of Pir Iqbal the Impaled*

HWORDE

N • *Hemisphere Eleven*

Nab Saheb and Denys X. Arbaris • *Bergmetal: Oro-Emblems of the Musical Beyond*

Yuu Seki • *Serial Kitsch*

www.ingramcontent.com/pod-product-compliance
Lightning Source LLC
Chambersburg PA
CBHW020438030426
42337CB00014B/1314